SECOND NATURE
CHANGES & CHALLENGES IN THE NEW ENVIRONMENT

The Air Out There

HOW CLEAN IS CLEAN

By Matthew Higgins

with Mark Stewart

NORWOOD HOUSE PRESS

All photos courtesy of Getty Images, except for the following:
Deposit Photos (6, 10, 14, 20, 22, 36, 40); Black Book Partners archives (18); Caroline Brown (27), Associated Press (31).

Front Cover: Deposit Photos

Special thanks to Content Consultant Ashley McDowell.

Library of Congress Cataloging-in-Publication Data

Higgins, Matthew.
  The air out there : how clean is clean? / by Matthew Higgins, Mark Stewart.
     p. cm. -- (Second nature)
  Includes bibliographical references and index.
  Summary: "This book helps young readers understand what happens every time
living things take a breath--physically, chemically and culturally. It
examines the science of air pollution, while discussing the hurdles
presented by globalization, politics and basic human need. The book also
separates fact from fiction when it comes to both manmade and natural
pollution"--Provided by publisher.
  ISBN-13: 978-1-59953-451-0 (library edition : alk. paper)
  ISBN-10: 1-59953-451-7 (library edition : alk. paper)
1. Air--Pollution--Juvenile literature. I. Stewart, Mark, 1960- II.
Title.
  TD883.13.H54 2012
  363.739'2--dc23
                              2011017623

Manufactured in the United States of America in North Mankato, Minnesota.
176N—072011

COVER: A dandelion blows away in a breeze. Should we be worried that our air might not be healthy enough to breathe some day?

Contents

Words in **bold type** are defined on page 46.

1 What's the Problem?
TOUGH TIME TO BREATHE EASY

Every time you draw a breath, your body interacts with the environment. Your lungs absorb a mixture of gases that we call "air," taking in what you need and getting rid of what you don't. Nitrogen and oxygen make up 99 percent of the air you breathe. The remaining one percent contains tiny amounts of 14 different gases. Along with the gases that make up the air you breathe, your body also absorbs water vapor, dust particles, plant spores, and **bacteria**. If there are pollutants in the surrounding environment—either manmade or from nature—your lungs will have to process those, too.

The human body is built to deal with almost anything contained in the air out there. That's good to know, because you breathe in and out around 1,000 times every hour. Clean air is important to good health, yet people who live in places where there are pollutants in the air can live healthy lives. At what point does air become *un*healthy? Environmental scientists search for answers to this question every day.

This baby needs help breathing because he suffers from asthma, a lung disease that can be made worse by polluted air.

to heat homes and cook food must be clean. And it is. However, natural gas leaves chemicals and soot after it is burned. The lesson here is that even clean energy sources can pollute air we breathe.

In these pages, you will see the challenges we face in keeping our air clean, as well as the ways we're trying to solve them. At first, these ideas may seem simple. But because so many things affect the balance between "dirty" and "clean" air, you will see why people devote their lives to the problem—and why there is so much work yet to be done.

THE CAUSES OF AIR POLLUTION

The quality of the air we breathe is closely connected to human activity. The activities with the greatest impact are the creation and use of energy. Right now, the world we live in is powered by fossil fuels—including oil, coal, and natural gas. When you ride a school bus, fry an egg, or flick on a light switch, you probably are using energy from one of these sources. You can smell the exhaust from the bus and you can see the blue flame under the frying pan (if you have a gas stove). Electricity is generated in power plants that often burn coal. You may not be able to see the chimneys from your home, but the smoke they produce is still mixing into the air.

Burning fuel adds dangerous elements to the air we breathe. For example, automobile engines that run on gasoline (a product of oil) pump hydrocarbons, nitrogen dioxide (NO_2), and carbon monoxide (CO) into the atmosphere. Hydrocarbons come from the unburned fuel that evaporates into the air. NO_2 can also affect the environment in the form of **acid rain**. CO is a poisonous gas.

Carbon dioxide (CO_2) is another by-product of cars. (We also make it whenever we exhale.) It's created when the carbon in the gasoline bonds with the oxygen in the air. Although CO_2 is not a toxic pollutant, environmental scientists believe that it may be a major factor in **climate change**.

In the Beginning

Where did the oxygen we breathe come from? We know that it built up in the atmosphere around 2.4 billion years ago. Scientists believe oxygen was produced by bacteria in the Earth's oceans. Until recently, there was no fossil evidence of why this happened when it did.

In 2009, researchers announced that they discovered a drop in the level of a metal called nickel in ocean water about 2.5 billion years ago. Nickel entered the water through volcanic eruptions. As the earth cooled and there were fewer eruptions, less nickel mixed with seawater.

High levels of nickel helped a different type of bacteria thrive. This bacteria produced methane, a poisonous gas. With less nickel in the water, oxygen-producing bacteria "took over." And the rest is history!

Power plants that use coal burn it to make super-hot steam. The steam goes through pipes to spin large turbines that are fitted with magnets. The spinning turbines create electricity, which makes its way into homes and businesses. Electricity itself is a very clean form of energy. However, the smoke that comes from producing it contains many of the same pollutants as car engines (including CO, CO_2, and NO_2). It also contains sulfur dioxide (SO_2), which can create air pollution and cause acid rain.

PEOPLE, PLANTS & ANIMALS

Millions of people live in places where they breathe air containing high levels of pollutants. The very young and the very old are the first to show the ill effects of this exposure. Young people tend to spend more time outside and also exert themselves more while running and playing. The lungs of older people may have suffered damage over a lifetime, so they don't function as well.

Nitrogen oxide and sulfur dioxide can damage lung tissue and make breathing very difficult. When the particles that come from smokestacks and car engines are inhaled, they can trigger asthma attacks or severe **bronchitis**. Even ozone, a gas that helps block the sun's radiation high in the atmosphere, can trigger breathing problems when it is present at ground level.

In cities such as Bangkok, Thailand, people sometimes wear masks because of poor air quality.

When nitrogen oxide and sulfur dioxide mix with water, the reaction can create carbonic acid. If this happens in the upper atmosphere, the carbonic acid falls from the clouds as "acid rain." Acid rain can eat away the marble in statues and buildings. When it falls on trees, plants, and soil, it puts the **ecosystem** under stress. When acid rain falls in lakes and streams, it changes the chemistry of the water. Some fish species cannot survive in the new conditions. This affects the whole food chain.

Most scientists believe that the impact of air pollution on land animals is not as powerful and direct. However, they are deeply concerned about rising temperatures and

The effects of air pollution include acid rain, which devastated this forest.

changing climates, which disrupt entire ecosystems. Most agree that **carbon dioxide emissions** contribute greatly to this problem. A study in 2009 showed that there is 35 percent more CO_2 in the atmosphere than there was a century ago. That's a big difference!

Almost everyone agrees that the air we breathe could and should be cleaner. Solving this problem is very tricky, however. It will almost certainly take personal sacrifices on the part of most people. Cleaner air will almost certainly cost us all more money, too. Will people be willing to make those sacrifices and spend that money? You can answer only for yourself. Hopefully, your answer is *Yes*…because what seems expensive now may look like a bargain in the years ahead.

Every Breath You Take

The air you breathe is a mixture of gases, including nitrogen and oxygen. Air may also contain natural substances, including water vapor, dust, and pollen. Pollutants such as sulfur dioxide may also be in the air. These are the gases you are likely to inhale with every breath:

GAS	SYMBOL	PERCENTAGE
Nitrogen	N_2	78.08%
Oxygen	O_2	20.95%
Argon	Ar	0.93%
Carbon Dioxide	CO_2	0.04%
Neon	Ne	Less than 0.01%
Helium	He	Less than 0.01%
Methane	CH_4	Less than 0.01%
Krypton	Kr	Less than 0.01%
Hydrogen	H_2	Less than 0.01%
Nitrous Oxide	N_2O	Less than 0.01%
Carbon Monoxide	CO	Less than 0.01%
Xenon	Xe	Less than 0.01%
Ozone	O_3	Less than 0.01%
Nitrogen Dioxide	NO_2	Less than 0.01%
Iodine	I_2	Less than 0.01%
Ammonia	NH_3	Less than 0.01%

WORLD VIEW

One way that scientists judge air quality is by tracking the amount of CO_2 released into the atmosphere. CO_2 emissions are a major contributor to **global warming**. According to the Carbon Dioxide Information Analysis Center, the world's total CO_2 emissions for 2007 were more than 29 million metric tons, or the weight equivalent to 29 million elephants.

CO$_2$ Emissions in 2007

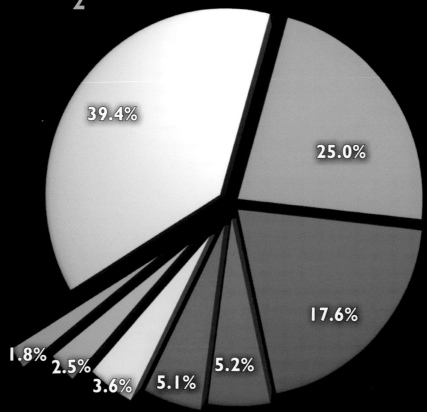

39.4%

25.0%

17.6%

1.8%

2.5%

3.6%

5.1%

5.2%

COUNTRY	TOTAL EMISSIONS *
China	6,538
United States	5,838
India	1,612
Russia	1,537
Japan	1,255
Germany	788
Canada	557
Rest of World	11,195

*Million metric tons of CO$_2$

NOTE: One metric ton of CO$_2$ is equivalent to the annual energy use of 422,542 homes.

2 How We Got Here

AIR POLLUTION THROUGH THE AGES

Human beings have been aware of air pollution since our early ancestors first sat by a campfire and breathed in the smoke. For most of human history, the greatest challenges to our air were natural. They included volcanic eruptions and forest fires. Both could choke the atmosphere with lung-burning, eye-watering pollutants—and in some cases, block out sunlight.

The volcanic dust from an eruption in Peru in 1601 led to **famine** in Russia, which is half a world away. In 1815, Mt. Tambora erupted in Indonesia. Falling ash ruined crops in villages more than 1,000 miles away, and more than 50,000 people starved to death. Elsewhere in the world, 1816 was called the "Year with No Summer." The sun

In the early days of human history, the major source of air pollution was erupting volcanoes.

could not cut through the volcanic dust filling the atmosphere from the Indonesian eruption in 1815. Crops failed, and livestock died across North America and Europe.

Natural air pollution still creates havoc today. In the summer of 2010, more than 800 wildfires burned near the Russian city of Moscow. By the time firefighters brought them under control, nearly 100 people had died from breathing the toxic air. At times, levels of carbon monoxide were seven times higher than the allowable limit. Earlier in 2010, a volcanic eruption in Iceland shot great clouds of ash across Europe. Fearing that this material would cause jet engines to fail, thousands of flights were cancelled. Travelers were stranded, and airlines lost millions of dollars each day until the clouds finally thinned to safe levels.

A GROWING PROBLEM

Not until large numbers of people began living close together in cold places did man-made air pollution become a concern. Five centuries ago in London, England, the burning of coal during the winter months filled the air with soot. More than 150,000 people lived in the city, and at times it was hard to breathe. This was true for rich and poor people alike—although the rich had the power to do something about it. Queen Elizabeth I ordered her people to cease burning coal when parliament was in session. The country's leaders needed a few smoke-free days to get their business done.

The Valley of Smokes

Los Angeles, California, is a city famous for its smog. Smog is a combination of two words: smoke and fog. It is caused when sunlight mixes with emissions from burning fuel. Smog is very dangerous for people with breathing problems.

Californians have been concerned about smog for more than 50 years. But it has been around Los Angeles much longer than that. In 1542, Spanish explorer Juan Rodriguez Cabrillo noted a strange, brownish haze over the area when he passed by on a ship. He called it the "Valley of Smokes." This smog was caused by the many campfires of the area's indigenous people, the Gabrielinos.

The problem then (and now) is that Los Angeles sits in a "basin" surrounded by high mountains. Smog hangs too low to clear the mountains, and there is not enough rainfall to "scrub" the air clean.

Smog often hangs heavy over Los Angeles.

This print shows a United States factory from the Industrial Revolution in the 1870s. Back then, people didn't yet realize that air pollution was so unhealthy.

By the mid-1800s, the air in London and other major cities around the world could be unbreathable at times. The Industrial Revolution had begun; factories were burning coal in huge quantities as they competed to make products quickly, cheaply, and in vast numbers. Factory workers lived nearby the factories in cramped housing. Not only were they around burning coal all day, they also burned it to heat their homes.

Scientists began pointing out the dangers of air pollution during this time, but governments didn't always listen to them. Officials were more concerned with making sure water was clean. This was because it was easier to see the pollution in water and to understand its effects on people. Only when air quality reached a crisis point (and people were dying) did the first laws controlling smoke go into effect in Europe and the United States.

In 1948, the English city of Coventry became the first to create a "smoke-free" zone. It covered 35 acres and 179 buildings. No coal was allowed to be burned by the businesses or residents in this area. Concern over air quality in the United States also began to grow in the 1940s and 1950s. By the mid-1960s, the U.S. Congress had created the Clean Air Act. This made the control of air pollution a federal responsibility and gave added power to the **Environmental Protection Agency (EPA)**.

Among the important steps that followed were laws that made drivers switch to unleaded gasoline. For more

Exhaust from tailpipes has long been one of the primary causes of air pollution.

than 50 years, lead was added to gasoline to help engines run more smoothly. Lead is very toxic when it enters the body. Millions of tons were released into the air each year in the form of exhaust from tailpipes. Leaded gas was outlawed in the U.S. during the 1980s and in Europe during the 1990s.

Another important law was one that made car companies use catalytic converters in their vehicles. The catalytic converter is a device that creates a chemical reaction among engine emissions before they leave a car's tailpipe. Since cars with catalytic converters only run on unleaded fuel, this helped phase out the use of leaded gas. Unfortunately, leaded gas is still used in many developing countries today, such as Algeria and Egypt.

THE BIG SMOKE

When a weather condition called an inversion happens in a place with poor air quality, the results can be deadly. Air close to the ground is almost always warmer than the air higher up. When the opposite is true, it is called an inversion—the warm ground air rises and traps the colder air beneath it. This also keeps polluted air closer to the ground.

The first days of December in 1952 were very cold in London. Coal fires from a million homes and thousands of businesses created a layer of soot, tar particles, and sulfur dioxide that hung over the city. On December 5, freezing air swept through city streets, and the thick smog sank to ground level for nearly five days. At times it was hard to see more than 200 feet. London had experienced conditions like this before, but in the days after it lifted, scientists realized this event was different.

Measurements showed that the air was 50 times dirtier than normal. In some places, the soot had combined with water vapor to form sulfuric acid. This is an extremely dangerous chemical to touch. Breathing it in can be fatal. For more than 4,000 people, it was. They died from a range of severe breathing difficulties in the days and weeks that followed. Over the next year, thousands more may have passed away as a result of health problems created by the "Big Smoke."

In 1952, an inversion helped create the "Big Smoke" that blanketed London.

3 If We Do Nothing

CAN WE SURVIVE WITHOUT CLEAN AIR?

Everyone agrees on the need to keep the air we breathe clean. But they *disagree* on two questions: Is clean air more important than other things that affect people's everyday lives, such as good jobs? And how clean is clean enough? The answers aren't always easy.

If Country A works hard to keep pollutants out of the air, it cannot "capture" that air and use it only for itself. The air on our planet is constantly moving and changing. If Country B, Country A's neighbor, has an air pollution problem, it won't be long before its dirty air begins to drift over and trigger environmental problems in Country A. Country A can ask Country B to clean up its act, but what if Country B won't? Or can't?

The name for this situation is **transboundary** air, and it is a real problem in many parts of the world—including North America. For many years, the smoke from factories in the northern part of the United States entered the atmosphere, where it mixed with water vapor and fell to earth in Canada as acid rain. In the 1970s, Canadian scientists began noticing changes in the environment,

Air pollution created in one area will eventually become a problem for neighboring regions, too.

including large numbers of dead fish in what they thought were unspoiled ecosystems. The cause was determined and Canada quickly passed laws to curb factory emissions. However, the United States was slower to act. It took many years for Canada to convince American companies that they were part of the problem. Not until 1991 did the two countries finally agree on a plan to tackle this problem.

THE EFFECTS OF GLOBALIZATION

Have you ever noticed that a lot of the "bargains" you see in stores are products made in other countries? If you believe that clean air is important, these bargains may "cost" much more than you think. In most parts of North America and Europe, there are laws to make sure companies don't pollute the air. It can be expensive to follow these rules—too expensive, in some cases, to make certain products close to home. When this happens, companies set up factories in places where the laws are not as strict. This helps to keep the cost of the product low.

Products *Made in China* are usually bargains, but the factories that make them are responsible for harmful air pollution.

is one reason you may see *Made in China* or *Made in India* on some low-priced items.

When a company in one country sets up a factory in other countries, this is called "globalization." Often, the people who work in the factories are very poor. They are glad to have the jobs. Air pollution may be a concern for them, but it is not their most pressing problem. For them, survival comes first, and healthy lungs come second.

Where you find one factory like this, you are likely to find hundreds more, or maybe even thousands. And this is where globalization—which is good in some ways because it supplies much-needed jobs around the world—is actually bad for the air we breathe. For every factory in North America and Europe that has cleaned up (or shut down), there are many more opening around the world releasing harmful pollutants into the atmosphere.

Today, many companies that used to make products in their home countries use factories in China. They do this

LONG WAY TO GO

The United States has made important strides in the fight for clean air. Most people believe things have improved greatly in just the past generation. This may be true, but there is a long way to go—the more we understand about the air we breathe, the more we know this is true.

For example, researchers now believe that air pollution causes more deaths in the U.S. each year than car accidents. A 2010 study also showed a link between air pollution and heart attacks, so the number of "air pollution deaths" may be even higher. We gladly spend billions of dollars making cars and roads safer. Only a small fraction of that amount goes toward reducing air pollution.

to save money on their manufacturing costs. But there is also a problem with this strategy. Chinese factories burn coal in ways that harm the air and contribute to global warming. That raises tough questions. Is it fair to demand that countries such as China shut down their factories? Can we ask them to pay their workers less—or fire some of them—so they can afford to use newer, cleaner, more expensive technology?

ADDRESSING CLIMATE CHANGE

The economies of countries such as China continue to grow. Because their air-quality laws are not very strict, they will pump more and more CO_2 and other pollutants into the atmosphere. The same is true in the United States, where there are no laws in place to prohibit CO_2 emissions. Most scientists think these emissions will speed up the process of climate change. If so, natural resources, including water, could be put at risk.

That is why many people supported the Kyoto **Protocol**. Under this plan developed by the United Nations, more

People everywhere celebrated the Kyoto Protocol, partly because it cracked down on the developed countries responsible for large CO_2 emissions.

than 150 countries agreed to reduce the emissions of **greenhouse gases** believed to cause global warming. They also agreed to find cleaner, more efficient ways of producing energy. Developing countries such as India were given extra time to comply.

Despite the excitement generated by the Kyoto Protocol, it did not produce strong results. World leaders acknowledged the need to reduce CO_2 emissions, but for many countries, including the U.S., their commitment ended there. Some felt the agreement didn't go far enough, and others believed they would be better off dealing with the problem on their own. Some countries that had to reduce their CO_2 emissions found an easy solution—they simply moved factories to countries where the rules did not apply. Environmental scientists learned that the fight for clean air had just begun.

SAVING THE SUGAR MAPLE

One day you may be telling your grandchildren about the sweet stuff kids used to pour over their pancakes and waffles. You will tell them it was collected in cans from special trees (below). They probably won't believe you, because there may not be many of these trees left. Sugar maples are among several tree species that are very sensitive to air pollution. In the U.S. and Canada, scientists have noticed that the top branches of sugar maples are dying. They believe it is due to pollutants in the air that cause acid rain. The same problem may also be causing lower syrup production.

4 Bright Ideas
MAKING THE AIR CLEANER

Wouldn't it be nice if we could just clean the air the way we wash our laundry? There are actually scientists and inventors looking at the problem of air pollution from this perspective. They hope to find ways to cleanse air of harmful substances.

The other plan of attack is to reduce the amount of elements released into the air. People who are concerned about the environment have been waging this battle for a long time. They are working with car manufacturers, oil companies, and other industry leaders to find ways to make businesses run cleaner and more effectively.

ELECTRIC CARS

Fighting against harmful emissions from automobiles has been a top priority among environmental scientists for more than a generation. Only recently, however, have carmakers become true partners in this battle. Their shared goal now is to create vehicles that burn little or no fossil fuel. Most people agree that soon almost all cars will depend on electricity as an energy source. Automobiles

The excitement over electric cars has already begun. In 2011, seven companies showed new models.

PURE AIR

One way to treat polluted air is with air purifiers. They can be used in enclosed "outdoor" spaces such as tunnels and underground parking garages. Great turbines located at ground level pull air out of these spaces and remove the particles and gases produced by cars and trucks. The same process brings fresh air into garages and tunnels.

Different filters are used for different jobs, but in some places, Mother Nature does the work. In Japan, "earth air-purifier" systems were introduced in the 1990s. They now sit atop dozens of structures. Polluted air is pumped up through specially designed rooftop gardens. The air is cleaned in the soil and root zones of the plants. The whole process takes around 30 seconds.

will carry large batteries that can be recharged at home and on the road. Don't be surprised one day to find that your neighborhood gas station has replaced its pumps with plugs!

For many car owners, that day has already come. Seven different companies produced electric cars in 2011, and soon every car manufacturer will offer their own models for sale. In some cities, including New York City, there are already fleets of electric buses. Have electric vehicles improved air quality? Anyone who grew up in the 1950s and 1960s will tell you they can already smell the difference. Indeed, it takes more than 20 of today's electric cars to produce the same amount of air pollution as the cars of their childhoods.

Cars that run on electricity have actually been around for over a century. In the early 1900s, they made up a large

Electric cars actually made their first appearances in the 1800s.

percentage of automobiles. In the years that followed, automakers began learning more about gas engines. This technology proved to be more efficient and effective, and electric cars were phased out.

Today, the main advantage of electric engines is that they do not emit pollutants. That does not mean they are 100 percent clean, though. Remember, the electricity used to recharge the batteries is produced in a power plant somewhere.

How quickly we get more electric cars on the road depends on solving serious problems. Right now, electric cars cost thousands of dollars more than regular cars. Will governments be willing to make up the difference with refunds or credits? The lithium-ion batteries in electric cars do not have as much range as a tank of gas, so drivers are afraid that they will run out of power between recharging stops. Who will build more charging stations for these drivers? Who will design better batteries? Each country is answering these questions in its own way. The U.S. government has pledged over $2 billion to help the electric car industry. In China, the government is spending six times that amount.

REDUCING CO$_2$ EMISSIONS

Efforts to reduce tailpipe emissions have succeeded because people decided it was important enough to make changes in the way they live. They are willing to spend a little more—and make sacrifices—in order to breathe easier. This convinced carmakers and oil companies to work toward the same goal.

Efforts to curb air pollution produced by industry have not been as successful. Businesses sometimes think twice about spending money to fix environmental problems because it cuts into profits. It may also mean that workers earn less or that some have to be fired. Those are hard sacrifices, and not everyone is willing to make them.

Sometimes it takes strict laws to make companies curb their emissions. In order to comply with these laws, companies turn to scientists to help them find workable solutions. One solution that has become popular is "scrubbing." There are different ways to scrub emissions, but all involve some kind of **filtering**.

The most common type of scrubbing uses water to filter out carbon contaminants and other chemicals. The latest scrubbers can remove up to 90 percent of CO_2 emissions and many other pollutants. Of course, then the company has to safely dispose of the dirty water, which can be very expensive. Some scientists are looking for ways to clean the water and use the material they remove for other purposes. One day, for instance, you may sit in a chair made from the pollutants removed from the air by scrubbing.

In Illinois, a project called FutureGen hopes to find a different solution. A special power plant will compress the CO_2 it produces and then send it through pipes more than a mile underground, where it will be held by layers of limestone and shale. This is the same way the earth "traps" natural gas deposits. Will FutureGen work? Some say it will be too expensive. Others feel that scrubbing is a better way to treat CO_2 emissions. But most believe that every bright idea deserves a chance.

The Montreal Protocol

In the battle to improve air quality, one of the great success stories is the banning of **chlorofluorocarbons** (CFCs). For many decades, CFCs were used in spray cans. In the 1970s, scientists discovered that when CFCs were exposed to sunlight in the middle stratosphere, they released chlorine atoms. These atoms created large "holes" in the ozone layer, a gas that protects living things from radiation. After meeting in Montreal, Canada, the countries of the world agreed to stop using CFCs. Many scientists believe the ozone holes will be repaired by the year 2050.

5 Trailblazers

These people are doing things to help keep the air clean today...and make the world better for tomorrow.

Guy Negre

Engineer

During the 1980s, Negre built high-performance engines for airplanes and race cars. In the 1990s, he invented a car engine that uses **compressed** air instead of gasoline or electricity. Soon the OneCAT, MiniCAT, and CityCAT engines may be coming to a street near you.

Matthew Johnson

College Professor

A high percentage of the energy used in the world goes toward heating, cooling, and **dehumidifying** buildings. This is mostly because air must be vented to avoid indoor air pollution. Johnson devised a way to clean this air so it can be reused. This could reduce energy costs by more than 20 percent.

Robin Chase
Entrepreneur

In 2000, Chase (right) started a car-sharing company called Zipcar. Drivers rent a car by the hour or by the day, but only when they need to drive somewhere. Thanks to Zipcar, roughly 500,000 people share fewer than 10,000 cars. That means greater use of public transportation and fewer cars on the road, all of which reduces air pollution.

Pamela Campos
Lawyer/Physicist

Growing up in Colorado, Campos saw the air quality in cities such as Denver get worse and worse. In 2011, she worked with lawmakers to create a new law that will force power plants in the region to change from coal to cleaner sources by 2018.

6 Field Tested

Improving air quality in large cities is one of the greatest challenges environmental scientists face. Each city has its own set of problems and its own "personality." In some places, strict rules must be enforced with drastic measures. In other places, everyone has to make small changes in their lives and work together as a team. The area in and around Salt Lake City, Utah, is known for its clean air and healthy lifestyle. In 2010, however, the people decided it could be even cleaner and healthier.

For one month, city residents took the Clear the Air Challenge. Twenty different organizations in Salt Lake City contacted friends, families, students, and workers and asked them to dramatically reduce the number of single-occupant car trips they took. If two people ride in one car instead of two, it cuts the amount of harmful emissions by half.

After a month, the results were amazing. People participating in the Clear the Air Challenge had taken 103,710 fewer single-occupant trips. That kept 2.1 million pounds (952,544 kilograms) of emissions out of the city's air. Many people continued to "double up" when they drove after the Challenge ended. The program is now being used as a model of success in other cities.

The Mormon Temple is one of Salt Lake City's most famous buildings. Thanks to the Clear the Air Challenge, views of it are incredibly scenic.

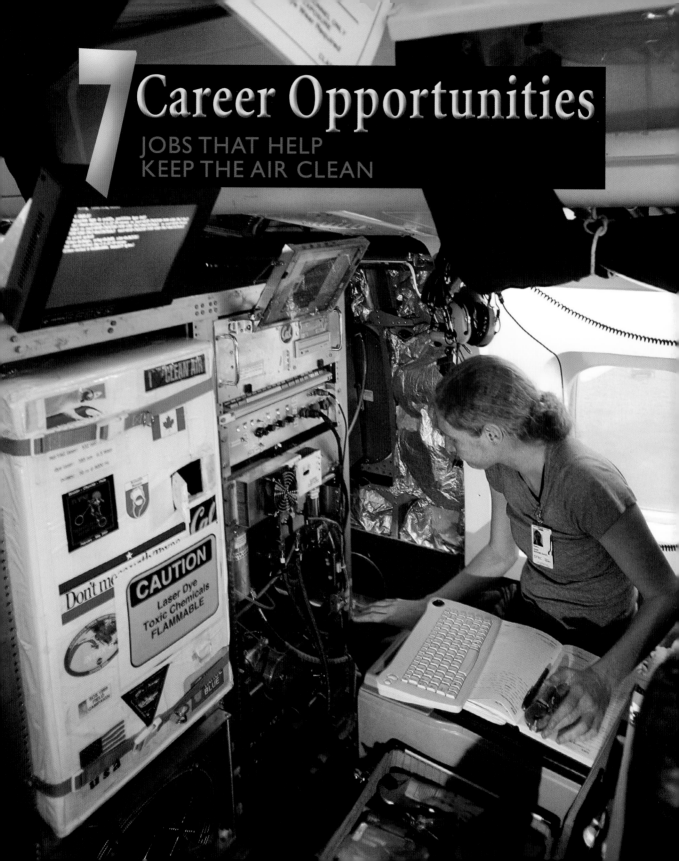

Young people who want to make a difference in the air we breathe will have many career choices in the future. Much of the work will be done in two areas: chemistry and engineering. Both of these fields offer a wide range of jobs for people with different interests and talents.

For example, atmospheric chemistry is the study of how the air we breathe responds to different conditions and how it affects living things. Many people in this field are looking for solutions to the complicated problems of air quality and climate change. When someone in government or industry has an idea to change or improve the way emissions enter the air, they turn to these scientists. Sometimes what seems like a brilliant solution can cause damage in some other part of the environment. Atmospheric chemists understand how **molecules** behave in the air, so they can perform tests and analyze theories while they are still on the drawing board.

Engineers enter the picture when ideas are ready to come off the drawing board. They design the things that change the way we deal with air pollution. There

A scientist checks equipment on a DC-8 jet that was turned into a flying laboratory used to study air pollution.

New Frontiers

Atmospheric chemistry is not an "earthbound" science. Although most people in this field focus on the issues and challenges facing our planet, more and more are turning their gaze to the stars. Once you understand how one planet's atmosphere works, you can analyze the atmospheres of other planets. As we search for planets in the universe that might contain life, atmospheric chemists will be able to answer some important questions.

Here on earth, they are still *raising* questions. The gases that make up the air we breathe were always thought to have been produced by volcanic eruptions billions of years ago. For the most part, that is true. However, in 2009, scientists found small amounts of two of these gases—xenon and krypton—trapped deep below the earth's surface. When the samples were analyzed, they did not resemble the xenon and krypton present in our air. They were closer to forms found in meteorites. This may mean that some of the air we breathe came from other worlds!

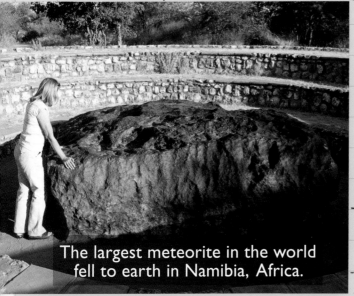

The largest meteorite in the world fell to earth in Namibia, Africa.

are dozens of different types of engineers, including environmental engineers. They use "pollution modeling" to study how waste products are disposed of. They also design new ways to keep dangerous materials out of the air, land, and water. Environmental engineers often work together with chemical engineers to find these solutions.

Automotive engineers look at ways to improve the efficiency of gasoline engines. They also design engines that run off of cleaner power sources. Industrial engineers explore ways to make factories "smarter." Part of their job is to design systems that will reduce a company's emissions.

While some engineers work on ways to limit the impact of fossil fuels on the air we breathe, others are working on ways to create energy from other sources. Mechanical engineers design and build machines that take the energy produced by wind and water and turn it into electricity. They already have some brilliant ideas on the drawing board—including a system of underwater "kites" that will capture the energy that drives the strongest ocean currents…and deliver it right to your home!

A WORLD WITHOUT OIL?

Not likely! As the world reduces the amount of oil used for energy, it will still need oil for other things. These products include plastics, **synthetic** fabrics (such as nylon), and lubrication for machine parts. All are made from petroleum, another name for oil as it is found underground. The people who turn oil into useful products are called petrochemical engineers. They use science and math to turn the complex molecules in oil into simpler substances. These substances can then be combined in different ways to make a variety of useful products. When the products are no longer needed, they can be recycled and broken down again to be made into other things.

8 Expert Opinions

When the best minds talk about the world's air supply, it's worth listening to what they say.

"When I was growing up in Los Angeles, I remember days when the air was too smoggy to go outside and play, and today we understand how crucial clean air is for the health of our kids and communities."
—*Antonio R. Villaraigosa, Los Angeles Mayor, on the importance of clean air*

"Students are looking to make the world a better place, and we need to do what we can to help."
—*Catherine Middlecamp, University of Wisconsin professor, on the next generation of environmentalists*

"After twenty years of cooperation, emissions causing acid rain have been cut in half."
—*Peter Kent, Canadian Environment Minister, on a 1991 agreement between his country and the United States*

"Three million people now die each year from the effects of air pollution—three times the number of deaths each year in automobile accidents...While only some motorists contribute to traffic fatalities, all motorists contribute to air pollution deaths."

—Bernie Fischlowitz-Roberts, environmental activist, on the role that drivers play in air pollution

"If it is possible for industry to both capture CO_2 and produce a product from the CO_2 that they can sell, then they will be much more interested."

—Komar Kawatra, Michigan Tech professor, on what it will take for businesses to become more committed to reducing air pollution

"The health effects of air pollution **imperil** human lives. This fact is well documented."

—Eddie Bernice Johnson, U.S. Congresswoman, on the dangers of dirty air

LEFT: Catherine Middlecamp
ABOVE: Bernie Fischlowitz-Roberts

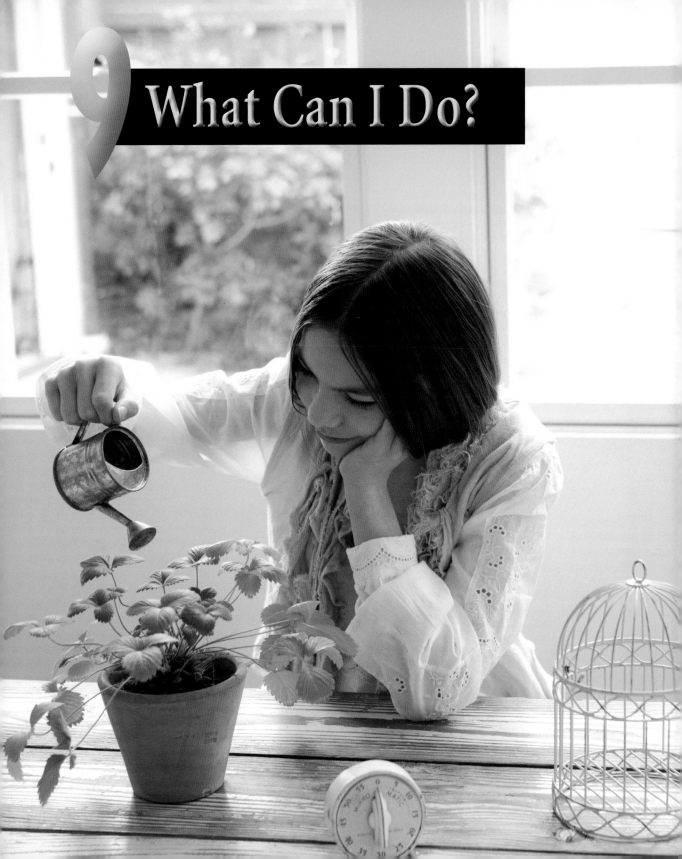

9 What Can I Do?

People who care deeply about the air we breathe hope that someday we'll live in a world that does not get its energy from fossil fuels such as oil and coal. Change will come slowly, but it *will* come. In the meantime, you can do your part to keep the air clean…and you can do so without leaving your home.

The energy source for televisions, computers, and other electric appliances may be a coal-burning power plant. Unfortunately, you cannot always control how your energy is made. However, if you turn them off when they are not in use, you will help cut emissions.

Cleaning the air indoors is also something you can control—with some help from Mother Nature. Plants and trees do an excellent job of turning bad air into good air. They absorb carbon dioxide and release oxygen as part of the growing process. Recently **NASA** scientists discovered that certain plants can also remove harmful pollutants from the air, including benzene and formaldehyde—two chemicals sometimes found in newer homes and buildings.

Different plants clean the air in different ways. Try arranging an Areca palm, money plant, and a snake plant (also called mother-in-law's tongue) together. The Areca palm cleans the air during the day. The snake plant produces oxygen best at night. And the money plant is good at taking chemicals out of the air.

Keeping plants inside is a good way to keep the air clean in

Glossary

Acid Rain—Rain with increased amounts of acid. It can be harmful to plants and animals.

Bacteria—Single-celled microorganisms that live in soil, water, or bodies of plants and animals.

Bronchitis—A condition marked by inflammation of tubes in the lungs.

Carbon Dioxide Emissions—Discharges of a colorless gas made up of one part carbon and two parts oxygen.

Chlorofluorocarbons—Gaseous compounds that contain carbon, chlorine, fluorine, and sometimes hydrogen.

Climate Change—A long-term change in weather conditions.

Compressed—Pressed together or flattened.

Dehumidifying—Removing moisture from the air.

Ecosystem—All the organisms, plants, and animals that make up a specific ecological area.

Environmental Protection Agency (EPA)—The government agency in the United States charged with protecting the environment.

Famine—An extreme shortage of food.

Filtering—Separating particles of a substance by passing it through some sort of barrier.

Global Warming—An increase in the earth's temperature caused by increases in greenhouse gases. There is debate among scientists about how much of global warming is caused by humans.

Greenhouse Gases—Gases that trap heat in the atmosphere, just like a greenhouse does during the winter.

Imperil—Put in grave danger.

Molecules—The smallest parts of a substance that keep all the same properties of that substance.

NASA—The abbreviation for the National Aeronautics and Space Administration, the government agency in the United States responsible for all space exploration.

Protocol—A document that outlines strict methods of reaching a goal.

Synthetic—Made in a laboratory, not in nature.

Transboundary—Extending across a border.

Sources

The authors relied on many different books, magazines, and organizations to do research for this book. Listed below are the primary sources of information and their websites:

The Atlantic Magazine	www.theatlantic.com
The Associated Press	www.ap.org
Los Angeles Times	www.latimes.com
National Geographic Magazine	www.nationalgeographic.com
The New York Times	www.nytimes.com
Time Magazine	www.time.com
Newsweek Magazine	www.newsweek.com

Resources

To get involved with efforts to help the environment, you can contact these organizations:

Environmental Protection Agency	www.epa.gov
National Center for Environmental Health	www.cdc.gov/nceh
National Institute of Environmental Health Sciences	www.niehs.nih.gov
Union of Concerned Scientists	www.ucsusa.org
Journal of Environmental Health	www.neha.org/JEH
Environment Canada	www.ec.gc.ca
National Renewable Energy Laboratory	www.nrel.gov

For more information on the subjects covered in this book:

Feinstein, Stephen. *Solving the Air Pollution Problem: What You Can Do.* Berkeley Heights, New Jersey. Enslow Publishers, 2010.

Gates, Alexander. *Encyclopedia of Pollution: Air, Earth, and Water.* New York, New York. Facts on File, 2011.

Haerens, Margaret. *Air Pollution.* Farmington Hills, Michigan. Greenhaven Press, 2011.

Index

Page numbers in **bold** refer to illustrations.

The Authors

DR. MATTHEW HIGGINS is an atmospheric scientist at the University of Colorado at Boulder. He specializes in Arctic climatology. Matt's doctorate is also from CU-Boulder, and he holds an undergraduate degree in chemical engineering from the University of Virginia. To help the environment, Matt often rides his bike to work.

MARK STEWART has written more than 200 non-fiction books for the school and library market. He has an undergraduate degree in History from Duke University. Mark's work in environmental studies includes books on the plants and animals of New York (where he grew up) and New Jersey (where he lives now).